The Horta Museum
Saint-Gilles, Brussels

Visited - March 18, 2003

D0097356

Françoise Aubry
Jacques Evrard, Christine Bastin, photographs

THE HORTA MUSEUM
SAINT-GILLES, BRUSSELS

Ludion

Victor Horta in the music room

Victor Horta was born into a large family in Ghent on 6 January 1861. His mother, Henriette Coppieters, was the second wife of Pierre Horta, a craftsman shoemaker who 'plied his trade with such superiority that for him it was an art' (*Mémoires,* p. 283). Pierre Horta also liked music and as a boy Victor was briefly drawn to playing the violin. But he was sent down from the Conservatoire de musique for lack of discipline and enrolled for architectural drawing at the Académie des Beaux-Arts. In 1878 he left for Paris, returning to Ghent two years later on the death of his father. In 1881 he married Pauline Heyse and set up home in Brussels, where he attended the Académie des Beaux-Arts while working to earn a living at the studio of the architect Alphonse Balat, whom he revered throughout his life. In his will, drawn up in 1944, Horta still felt the need to acknowledge the debt he owed his master. It is thanks to Balat that, on the basis of only three houses built in Ghent in 1885, the young man was commissioned in 1889 to design a small pavilion to house the monumental sculpture by Jef Lambeaux, *Les Passions humaines* (Parc du Cinquantenaire in Brussels). 1890 saw the birth of his only daughter, Simone. In his memoirs, written from 1939, he expresses his deep love of this child, of whom he was given custody after his divorce in 1906.

Hôtel Tassel: bel-étage landing

missions – a monument to Alfred Solvay in the courtyard of the factory at Couillet and the family tomb at the Ixelles cemetery – were followed by the conversion of the mansion at La Hulpe, the construction of a beautiful *hôtel de maître*, 224 avenue Louise (1894) and of a mansion at Chambley (in French Lorraine) for baron Henry de Wangen, Solvay's son-in-law (1897).

Still in 1894, the lawyer Maurice Frison, with whom Horta had become firm friends, commissioned him to build his house at 37 rue Lebeau in Brussels, a commission which seems to have caught the attention of the then deputy burgomaster, Charles Buls. Without running any competition at all, the city of Brussels commissioned Horta to design a *jardin d'enfants* (kindergarten) in the Marolles quarter (40 rue Saint-Ghislain). In this same popular district of Brussels, Horta designed an important building: the Maison du peuple for the Belgian Workers' Party (1895–1899). In his Memoirs he confirms that he was chosen for 'his aesthetic style' (*Mémoires*, p. 43) and not for his political ideas, 'whatever they might be'. Horta's sympathies were obvious: he had taught in the 'section d'Art' at the old Maison du peuple in rue de Bavière and was on friendly terms with party intellectuals such as Max Hallet, Léon Furnémont (for whom he would later build) and Emile Vandervelde (who was subsequently to play an important role in managing the Palais des Beaux-Arts).

We do not know why Edmond Van Eetvelde turned to Horta. The secretary of the Independent State of the Congo wanted a house in a style 'to suit everybody': a family house with huge reception areas in one of the most attractive quarters of Brussels, avenue Palmerston. Horta responded with a creation at the extremes of banality, 'my

The Maison du peuple, place Emile Vandervelde, Brussels

After years of struggle, Horta's career suddenly took off. Two friends, Eugène Autrique and Emile Tassel, whom he got to know from the Masonic lodge 'Les Amis Philantropes', to which he had been admitted in 1888, each commissioned him to build a small *hôtel de maître* (266 chaussée de Haecht in Schaerbeek and 6 rue Paul-Emile Janson in Brussels). Horta attained the goal he had set himself, 'to create a personal work in which constructive, architectural and social rationalism meet' (*Mémoires*, p. 13). It is thanks to a friend of Tassel, the engineer Charles Lefébure, secretary to Ernest Solvay, that Horta was introduced to the Solvay family in 1894. The first two small com-

boldest design so far' (*Mémoires*, p. 78). Following the Tervueren exhibition in 1897, Van Eetvelde was knighted and immediately commissioned an extension to his private mansion (1899).

With the Hôtel Tassel, Horta gained almost immediate recognition from both architects and the general public for his innovative boldness, yet it was not until the *Libre Esthétique* exhibition in Brussels in 1897 that a wider public discovered his qualities as an interior designer and decorative artist. At the exhibition, he showed a wool carpet created for Anna Boch, stained-glass windows and a sideboard for the Hôtel Van Eetvelde and a dining-room table and chairs for the Hôtel Solvay.

The increased number of commissions between 1893 and 1898 enabled Horta to purchase two plots of land in the rue Américaine in Saint-Gilles, where he built his

Hôtel Van Eetvelde: octagonal hall

own house and studio. His art quickly developed and at the turn of the century he abandoned the demonstrative use of metal structures: the Hôtel Aubecq (520 avenue Louise, 1899), the Roger residence (459 avenue Louise, 1901), the Dubois residence, (80 avenue Brugmann, Forest, 1901) and the Max Hallet residence (346 avenue Louise, 1902) are outstanding for the beauty of their stonework.

But Horta did not abandon the use of metal structures in the frontages of large stores, where they were absolutely essential to open up the buildings as much as possible to the street. The commissions for A l'Innovation (rue Neuve, 1900 and chaussée d'Ixelles in Brussels, 1903, and on the Meir in Antwerp, 1906), the Grand Bazar Anspach (rue de l'Evêque in Brussels and in Frankfurt am Main, 1903), the Waucquez department store (now the Centre belge de la Bande dessinée, 20 rue

The Waucquez department store in Brussels

des Sables in Brussels, 1906) probably lost him some favour among his private clientele: in the light of the department store customers, his style as a bearer of the avant-garde image was no longer so exclusive.

Horta divorced in 1906 and two years later married a young Swedish gymnastics teacher, Julia Carlson.

Gradually Horta's career began to change direction as he devoted more time to teaching. In 1893 he had become Professor of Architecture at the Université Libre de Bruxelles, a post he resigned in 1911 after a disagreement with the academic authorities about the university's planned construction of new buildings. The following year, Horta became professor at the Brussels Académie des Beaux-Arts, and in 1913 he was elected principal for three years. He wanted to reform how architecture was taught and met with great hostility from some of his colleagues. These activities were interrupted by the First World War. Having left to attend a conference in London in 1915, he was unable to return to Belgium. Forced of necessity to earn his living, he went to the United States, where he gave lectures. He returned in 1919 and sold his house and studio. After these years of enforced exile, he had to face up to a difficult situation. He had to continue with the jobs he had already started: the Musée des Beaux-Arts in Tournai (1903–1928), the Brugmann hospital at Jette (1906–1923), the Gare Centrale (1912 – completed by Maxime Brunfaut between 1946 and 1952) and to fight to prove that he was still a great architect. In 1919, Horta submitted his preliminary plans for building a Palais des Beaux-Arts. The Belgian State rejected the plan, considering it too costly. It was relaunched in 1922 thanks to the intervention of Henri Le Bœuf and to the creation of the 'Société du Palais des Beaux-Arts', whose paid-up capital

The Musée des Beaux-Arts in Tournai

The Central Station, Brussels

was guaranteed by the Government. The colossal architecture of the Palais des Beaux-Arts was long underrated, probably because of the formal, classicizing language inspired by the architecture of the Place Royale, and of the discreet layout below the Place des Palais. However complex his situation after the First World War, Horta did not suffer from any lack of recognition; in 1925, he built the Pavillon

The Palais des Beaux-Arts, Brussels

d'Honneur de la Belgique as part of the exhibition of Decorative and Industrial Modern Art in Paris. The following year he presided over the panel for the international competition to design the Palace of the League of Nations in Geneva and was appointed *officier de la Légion d'honneur*. He was made a baronet in 1932 by King Albert I. Sadly, in 1939 and 1946, towards the end of his life, he destroyed most of his archives and drawings, while paradoxically also regretting the fact that he had never taken the trouble to publish his works.

'To each epoch, its art. To art, its freedom.' *(Der Zeit ihre Kunst. Der Kunst ihre Freiheit.)*

This motto, which is displayed on the frontage of the Secession House built by J.M. Olbrich in Vienna in 1898, shows the desire to which Art Nouveau was the response: the desire to break away from imitating styles of the past, to develop an art that reflected the sensitivities and way of life of a particular society, the extreme individuality of the artist dreaming of inventing an original language that would ensure the absolute harmony of the ornamentation of life.

The private home became the framework for an aesthetic experience for a new middle class with its newly acquired wealth in commercial or industrial enterprises. Art Nouveau was thus adopted by progressive people who took care to assert their modernity before it became widespread throughout all social classes or a transient fashion item. The word was spread by images displayed in decorative arts magazines and in commerce (department stores or 'magasins d'art').

Art Nouveau transformed the object, whether it was produced by a craftsman with traditional knowledge handed down over centuries or by industry. In the second half of the century there was intense debate between the supporters of the craftsman and those in favour of the first steps taken in industrial design. Henry Van de Velde, who 'converted' to the decorative arts in 1893 and was artistic adviser for industry and craft in Weimar in 1901, claimed to be the first to come out in defence of the machine (*Déblaiement d'art,* 1894), proclaiming that it would one day be the start of a new aesthetic.

There are numerous facets to Art Nouveau: from the exuberant ornamentation of Gaudi in Spain to the rustic simplicity of Serrurier-Bovy or the Japanese style of Mackintosh in Glasgow. The style was born, developed and died between 1893 and 1910. Initially based on the use of the arabesque and naturalist decoration, by the turn of the century it was gradually becoming more geometric. Just as a plant could be adapted more or less faithfully, the abstract curve expressed vital energy, growth and blossoming. To study the plant was also to understand the constructional system behind architecture as well as the object. Collections of models abound, bearing evocative titles such as *L'étude de la plante, son application aux industries d'art* ('The study of the plant, its application to the art industries') by Maurice Pillard-Verneuil (1900).

Art Nouveau aimed to embellish life's setting for both aesthetic and moral reasons. The competition to furnish workers' homes as part of the Liège Exhibition in 1905 demonstrates the wish felt at the time to give the worker a home worth coming back to. Commenting on the interior by Serrurier-Bovy, Jules Destrée evoked an 'impression of freshness, of health, joy and energy', Art Nouveau being seen as an antidote to the temptations of the 'bar'. Ten years earlier, Horta's construction of the Maison du Peuple also had a philanthropic aim: to open up an airy, light-filled space to people living in the slums. The choice of the Workers' Party also had its origins in the quest for a style that would deter the conservative middle classes.

Banister detail: mahogany knot

The family room on the bel étage

In 1898 Horta bought two plots of land, 23 and 25 rue Américaine, where he built his house and studio. He submitted his application for planning permission to the Commune of Saint-Gilles on 10 August 1898. Because they were two distinct plots and to preserve its intimacy, he immediately chose to have the house and studio clearly separate, a separation immediately obvious from the two different façades: the house is slightly broader (6.69 m) than the studio (5.81 m). Horta 'cheats' slightly by allowing the servants' stairs to encroach on the plot for the studio. The three stairwells form a hub at the heart of the two plots and make it possible for the masters of the house, the servants and the workmen to have

separate routes. In 1906, Horta divorced and decided to extend the two buildings on the garden side. Perhaps it was mainly to please his daughter Simone that he created an apartment for her with winter garden and terrace on the 2nd floor. Be that as it may, it is certain that this extension meant he could add a salon and a small dining room on the bel étage, a set of wardrobes and a larger dressing room on the first floor and an additional office on the ground floor of the studio. Shortly afterwards, in 1908, Horta enlarged the sculptors' studio in the cellar, adding what he called a 'sunken glazed courtyard'. He dug this new cellar in the garden and fitted it with a zinc roof with a lantern and two skylights. From then on it was no longer possible to reach the garden from the studio. In 1911 Horta submitted another conversion application; he wanted to convert part of the ground floor of the studio to a garage. He changed the ground level and replaced the large glazed frame, protected by an iron grille, with a wooden door. This alteration would be short-lived, however, because on his return from the United States in 1919 he sold the house and the studio to two different owners. The studio was converted into a middle-class home. In 1961 the house was again up for sale, and the architect Jean Delhaye, a former student of Horta who had also worked with him, persuaded the burgomaster of Saint-Gilles to put steps in motion to acquire the house. The Commune imposed one condition: that the State should classify it as a historic monument so that the restoration work would be subsidized. In 1963 Victor Horta's house and studio became the first listed Art Nouveau buildings in Brussels.

The Horta Museum opened in 1969. The work was very onerous and complex because of the plan: to convert the first floor into offices to be rented out; to create a caretaker's apartment; to provide offices for a curator, exhibition rooms (on the garden side of the 2nd floor), and a library open to the public (on the street side of the 2nd floor); while complying with the safety standards applicable for any place open to the public. The authenticity of the architecture did suffer as a result of the work directed by Jean Delhaye, but at the time it was generally thought that that was the price that had to be paid for saving the monument. The Maison du Peuple had just been demolished (1965–1966) and since 1950 the stones of the Aubecq residence had been scattered everywhere.

While the work was being carried out, Jean Delhaye set about finding furniture. Horta had got rid of his furniture and, although the décor and stained-glass windows had been preserved, the house was empty. The most important items were bought from the owners of two houses in Renaix: the Carpentier and Dopchie houses. Then, thanks to the 'Amis du Musée Horta' founded in 1982 by Mmes Renée Delhaye and Jacqueline Soyeur, the museum received regular donations. In 1999 the Jean and Renée Delhaye Foundation gave in trust the original furniture of the bel-étage dining room and salon.

The studio was bought by the Commune in 1973. Its previous

'Anna Boch' chair

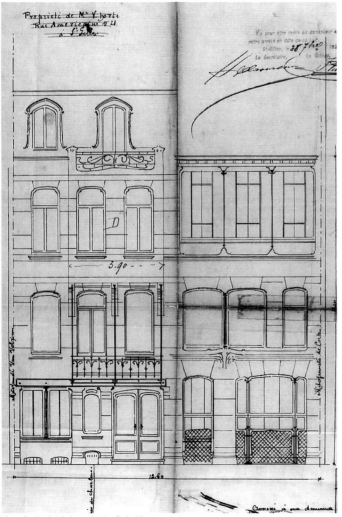

occupants had carried out major alteration work, so it is now in the process of being restored. In 1992, Madame Martine Wille, who chairs the Horta Museum's board of directors, appointed Barbara Van der Wee to draw up a full restortion plan. The most important works include reinforcing the main stairway (which was collapsing due to the great number of visitors); refitting the window and grille on the ground floor of the studio and the sculpture studio; fully restoring the roofs and façades at the rear of the building, the winter garden, the main stairwell and salon murals, the stained glass of the lantern (dismantled and releaded), and creating the exhibition halls in the cellars and a cloakroom and bookshop on the ground floor of the studio.

These works have been carried out thanks to the combined assistance of patrons (Société générale de Belgique, CBR and Union Minière) and the following authorities: the Bruxelles-Capitale Region for restoring the listed sections and the Communauté française for converting the studio cellars and ground floor into a museum.

In 2000, the Horta Museum was included in Unesco's list of world heritage sites.

Plan submitted with the application for building permission

Ground-floor studio railings (restored by the architect Barbara Van der Wee)

The link between these two architects, one restoring the ramparts at Carcassonne and the castle of Pierrefonds, the other creating the Hôtel Tassel, is not immediately apparent. The point they have in common is rationalism: 'setting aside certain prejudices, taking reason as the only guide' (XIII. Entretien, p. 142). Victor Horta carefully read Eugène Viollet-le-Duc's *Entretiens sur l'Architecture* (published in Paris in two parts in 1863 and 1872) and in many respects his work seems to illustrate the proposals put forward in these texts.

Firstly, architecture should meet a demand for the truth: 'being true to the plan means meeting exactly and scrupulously the conditions imposed by a need. Being true to the building processes means using materials for their qualities and properties' (X. Entretien, p. 451). Horta said that he created house-portraits, in other words houses totally adapted to their owners' particular way of life. He did not disguise the materials: stone is stone, wood is wood. And each material is worked according to its nature but with an eye towards general harmony. Horta knew that the agile and nervous movement that he imparted to the wrought-ironwork was not suitable for timber, whose shapes had to be fuller if the grain of the material was to be accentuated. When taken together, all the shapes create a resonant harmony.

Viollet-le-Duc rebelled against the metal skeleton of a building because 'as soon as the public sees iron being used as a principal structural means, they are immediately inclined to compare this structure to those used in railway stations, markets or factories' (XIII. Entretien, p. 132). Horta's architecture contributed greatly to smashing this association between iron and industrial architecture, although the prejudice continued to hold sway even among

Brass standard lamp

some of his clients. Thus Mme Van Eetvelde found that there was something 'common' about modernism (particularly because of its exposed building materials, the main one being iron; *Mémoires,* p. 79).

Viollet-le-Duc also railed against the tyranny of symmetry, stating that respecting a principle of unity and harmony did not necessarily imply symmetry. It was a mistake to insert similar windows into a façade regardless of the extremely varied uses of the rooms in a building. The architect distorts art and 'stifles its most noble quality of freedom to express its needs, its tastes and its individuality' (x. Entretien, p. 478). The façades of Victor Horta's house and studio bear witness to this quest for freedom.

The transcription of one of Viollet-le-Duc's proposals may be somewhat literal: the French architect suggested he drew inspiration from the network of English gothic arches to cover a void, replacing the stone with iron (XIII. Entretien, p. 134). Horta used this type of 'flying buttresses' for the glass roof that encloses the light source above the main stairway in the Hôtel Solvay. But led by his desire to let light into the heart of the building, he replaced the panes between the ribs of the building with American glass.

Viollet-le-Duc rejected eclecticism and wanted an art to be born for his time, giving shape to the new construction techniques developed as a result of the rapid industrial expansion. He would have to wait for the second decade of the century for his wish to be fulfilled; then, the engineer was no longer the only champion of progress, the only one who had technical knowledge. As Viollet-le-Duc had wished (XII. Entretien, p. 74), the qualities of the artist and of the scholar united in Victor Horta to give birth to a new art form.

Detail of the ironwork

THE FAÇADES

By designing two different façades for the house and the studio, Horta respected the character of the plots in the rue Américaine. The two adjacent plots gave him the width he needed to build a medium-sized town house, but the proportions would not have been very harmonious because of communal building restrictions that imposed a maximum height.

The two façades are in Euville and Savonnière stone with a blue stone base, making them look as though they are rooted in pavement made in the same material. This impression of being 'rooted' is accentuated by the curved profile of the stone. By using stone, Horta increased construction costs: middle-class houses were usually made of brick, stone being used solely for the doorsills and the base.

The façades are real proof of the opportunities presented by metal structures. In traditional architecture, the solids and the voids have to be superimposed to ensure the building is stable. This is not the case with the studio façade. Above the stone pillar between the entrance door and the window, a cast iron column leads to the first floor. At this level, the stone pillar between the windows is supported by the very flat stone arch of the ground-floor window, an arch that rests on two slender cast-iron supports. The second floor is almost entirely glazed, the two small columns placed on a projecting stone string-course supporting a metal lintel beneath the cornice. Another lintel crosses right through the façade between the ground floor and the bel étage of the house. This lintel, which is an I-shaped metal girder, has a dual purpose: to bear the load of the masonry and to anchor the balcony of the bel-étage floor. One of the innovations that Horta introduced is to combine two balconies with a bow window: the stone consoles that support the corbelled construction of the bow window are matched by a metal element making it possible to fix a suspended tie-rod for the balcony. The latter is extended over the main doorway to form a canopy, its floor being made of glass tiles to admit light.

Horta's name is associated with a whiplash line, the nervous arabesque of wrought-ironwork. But he also liked stone, to such an extent that at the end of his life he had no hesitation in claiming that 'luckily the warmth of the stones was all he needed to make him happy' (*Mémoires*, p. 60). When working with stone, he had a sculptor's instinct. All the cuts in the stones are studied and there are plaster scale models, made in the studio cellars, of those that were treated like sculptures. Horta thus ensured that the craftsman was absolutely faithful to the model:

The bow window on the first floor of the house

Balcony of the bel étage and detail of the metal consoles beneath the bow window

Detail of the sculpted stone beneath the studio first-floor window

each craftsman (carpenter, caster, stonecutter) was given three-dimensional models. These left the studio cellars in their thousands. A few that have miraculously survived are exhibited there today.

The stone that receives the small cast-iron column on the first floor of the studio spreads out in gentle waves that incorporate the aquatic castings from the window sill. Thus in this façade, with its 'monastic simplicity', as Horta described it (*Mémoires,* p. 71), this heavily worked stone has an extraordinary impact. The stone element often provides the 'broad back' to bear the load and the metal element ends in a tendril: wherever the two materials meet is seen as an opportunity to play sophisticated games with form.

The careful treatment of each detail – including the ventilation holes that have been made into

Studio letter box

decorative motifs – does not prevent the whole from looking instantly harmonious. Thus the façade of the house can be read as a landscape. Horta transposes nature, a major source of inspiration for the protagonists of Art Nouveau, into an almost abstract ornamental language: the grass motif in the groundfloor grille, the bog iris in the balcony and the dragonfly with wrought-iron wings and silhouetted body in the stone at the centre of the bow window.

The colours, although subtle, have an important role to play in the composition: the yellowy-white and grey-blue of the stones, the brown of the varnished oak and the pitch pine of the panelling, the pink of the granite stringcourse and ochre of the metal sections (this colour was rediscovered during a stratigraphic examination of the iron work). In his *Mémentos,* Horta recalls that 'he was laughed at out-of-hand' when he dismissed black as the 'natural' colour for iron (p. 306).

The rear façades display barely any distinguishing features: they are the colour of the sand used to make their coating.

The rear façades from the garden

Once over the threshold, the visitor finds himself at a double-entrance door, where he is directed either to the studio (a section of the panelling on the right sliding door) or towards the cloakroom. By strategic use of the doors, the cloakroom can be cut off totally, making it into a visiting room, or alternatively a corridor can be skilfully created for the servants or tradesmen going to the servants' quarters. Horta adapted the traditional plan of the middle-class house on the bel étage, which had the cellar kitchen occupying the street side, preventing any even remotely spacious access at street level. Some white marble steps led to the bel étage comprising three linked rooms with a corridor alongside, and a staircase led to the other floors. The central section of these houses was generally rather dark, whereas Horta placed the cellar kitchen on the garden side under the dining room and ran the main rear staircase behind a stained-glass double door. He thereby created an entrance that lends itself well to reception functions while preserving the intimacy of the house.

Double door with stained glass between the hall and the foot of the stairs

Small circular window in the stairwell

For the double door that lets light in to the foot of the stairs, he used two panes of eye-catching American glass. This type of glass, which is found again in the lantern above the stairwell, had been invented in the United States by the Tiffany and La Farge glassworks in the 1880s. The glass is coloured with metal oxides and displays a chenille or undulated pattern achieved by pressing a roller embossed with motifs and reliefs onto the glass while it is still hot. It is dichroic, its colours changing depending on the intensity of the light, and is beautiful to look at from either side. Manufacture of this exceptionally high-quality glass ceased after the First World War. American glass is an essential element for creating the atmosphere in the houses designed by Horta,

Foot of the staircase on the ground floor

Banister and couch armrest

which practically cease to have any urban feel. The inhabitant or the visitor is bathed in the light of the undergrowth, of the seabed or of radiant summer days. The shapes themselves reinforce this impression, evoking the vital driving force behind nature.

But in the Horta house, this poetry of shape and light does not preclude the quest for comfort.

Right from the design stage, he incorporated new technologies – electric light, central heating – in such a way as not to disturb the harmony of the décor. These techniques sometimes result in a new aesthetic: for example the flanged radiator installed vertically at the foot of the staircase. Heating was needed here to take the chill off the air from the street. A cast-iron radiator would have been too cumbersome. So Horta got hold of an industrial radiator, which he installed vertically, making it into a column, while not forgetting to give it a curve by modifying the shape of the flanges from top to bottom. What is more, he encased the radiator with four small, slender columns linking the base to the canopy to ensure harmony of shape and to support the arch beneath the staircase landing. Horta also created lamps using the bulb invented by Edison in 1879; the electric bulb becomes a flower at the end of a stem, which often grows around a supporting structure like a climbing plant. Sometimes he made a decorative object of the electric cable from which the glass corollas hang. The transition from gas to electricity that took place in the 1890s also made it possible to lighten considerably the palette of colours used to decorate the interior. Gas was very dirty, making it essential to choose dark wallpaper or paint. With the advent of electricity, Horta was able to choose shades of white, pink, yellow, orange. In the stairwell, the mural painted white with pink stripes was very reminiscent of Carrara marble, an effect faded today by the patina that has developed over time. The coloured strips of the mural painting prepare the eyes for the marble stripes that form the dado of the dining room walls.

Foot of the stairs with radiator column

The basin in the axis of the first flight of stairs was originally a base for a group sculpted by Pierre Braecke: the heads of the two female statues stood out against the background of a stained-glass window, placed there to provide light for the servants' stairway. Horta used the stairwell topped with a stained-glass lantern as a source of light for the heart of the house, thus maximizing the light and overcoming the major inconvenience of the land being divided into deep parcels. The walls of the stairwell are inset with alcoves providing the servants' staircase with light. Until the lift was installed in the servants' stairwell during the 1960s' restoration, the two stairwells shared light sources and the colour of the stained-glass windows had not been blocked out as it is today.

The second flight of the main staircase leads to a white marble landing which, in this very open space, was treated like a cosy corner. Heavy velvet curtains were hung from gilt brass rails and two vents behind a grille emitted heat from a radiator concealed behind the couch in the music room. Horta and his wife could wait there before going in to dine.

Bel-étage landing pillar (with lamp)

The source of light in the stairwell

In the conversions carried out in 1906, the bel étage comprised only the music room, the landing and the dining room flanked by a pantry, an arrangement that accentuates the extravagance of the stairwell. The latter took up half the width of the music room, lending great style to the house. The spaces of the salon and the stairwell are interchangeable. To obtain this result, Horta used metal spans which, in a system comparable with that of gothic architecture, rest on a pillar of Belgian marble. The main span is the one in the music room, one side resting on the party wall and the other on the upright girder, thereby avoiding the need to build a transverse load-bearing wall. By opening up the heart of the house, Horta creates an explosion of space with multiple perspectives. Here fluidity prevails over the rigidity of enclosed spaces in traditional architecture.

In the music room the wall is divided into three horizontal sections: mahogany panelling in the lower section, 'jaspé' silk in the centre and a painting on canvas for the upper section. Golden butterflies embellish the attachments for the picture-hanging rods. Horta had a very astute taste for combining various materials of contrasting colours and textures that reflected his collections of oriental art. Today the house looks much barer than it did originally. It is rather hard to

View of the bel étage looking toward the dining room

36

imagine numerous oriental carpets coexisting with the eye-catching décor imagined by Horta.

The design of the dining room bears witness to an irrepressible boldness, for here Horta was his own master. As building material, he used the white enamelled bricks originally bought for the rear façade. Here the architecture seems to espouse the rational designs developed by Viollet-le-Duc. The décor springs out of the material itself without any attempt at disguise. Nevertheless, Horta felt obliged to 'modify' this ostentatious

Bel étage: music room

Detail of the panelling in the glass door of the dining room

simplicity by using precious woods, marbles and bevelled glass for the doors, 'expensive padding', as he described it (*Mémoires,* p. 72). The plaster bas-reliefs by Pierre Braecke provide the high point for the aristocratic décor of the space. Their meaning is still rather a mystery, apart from the gilded bottom bas-relief above the sideboard, which represents the arts. The muse in the foreground is the incarnation of architecture and holds a scale model of the Hôtel Aubecq, which Braecke also worked on. Originally, the dining room was bathed in light. The construction of the morning room on the garden side gave it a totally different feel: that of a place where the cult of the arts is practised daily.

Two doors open on either side of the sideboard, the one to the left leading off to the office, the one to the right towards the servants' staircase. The sideboard itself incorporates a serving hatch and a gas fire. As well as heating the dining room, the latter also warmed the plates by means of a metal plate built in on the office side. Another example of the desire to make everyday life more comfortable can be seen in the materials chosen for the floor. The Hungarian oak parquet is treated like a wooden carpet, with none of the inconvenience of taking care of wool. Horta reserves the marble mosaic for the circumference, as it is so cold on the feet in winter.

Bas-reliefs by Pierre Braecke in the dining room

Detail of the movable screen between the dining room and the salon

Bruxelles, Saint-Gilles - Musée Horta (a.s.b.l.).
1898-1901 - Hôtel Van Eetvelde, 2 Avenue Palmerston, Bruxelles.
Détail du bureau.
Architecte : V. Horta (1861-1947).

Brussel, Sint-Gillis - Hortamuseum (v.z.w.).
1898-1901 - Woning Van Eetvelde, Palmerstonlaan 2, Brussel.
Detail van het kantoor.
Architect : V. Horta (1861-1947).

Photo Jean Delhaye.

The salon on the garden side was densely furnished and decorated. Like the wing chair and dining-room table and chairs, Horta had intended to show the three-door display cabinet at the Exhibition of Decorative Arts in Turin in 1902. It cost Horta a great deal to create these items of furniture intended for such a prestigious exhibition. Being unable to sell them, he took them back and used them in his own interior after having made a few modifications.

The dining room seen from the garden side

Detail of the mosaic in the dining room

The garden side salon

Detail of a top of the Turin display cabinet

On the first floor, Horta's main
priority was to create an intimate
and comfortable atmosphere in the
family room and the bedroom. The
rooms skirt round the stairwell,
each with its own access. Originally
the boudoir and the bedroom were
separated by a screen containing
cupboards. Like those on either side
of the bedroom fireplace, these
proved to be superfluous when the
house was extended in 1906. The
bedroom was then extended by
a small room containing three cupboards and the entire inside wall
of the bathroom was fitted with
wardrobes and drawers. In the bathroom, three doors fitted with mirrors open onto a toilet on the left
and the bath on the right. The small
bathroom had a second exit to the
servants' staircase. During the conversion work, Horta changed the
passage between the bedroom and
the bathroom, moving it to the left
and installing a urinal in the space
between the doors.

The first-floor salon with Carpentier carpet

The family room

Bed of the first-floor bedroom

Bed of the first-floor bedroom

The guest-room

The second floor was taken up with
a guest-room on the street side and
Simone Horta's apartment on the
garden side. The guest-room is an
attic room, the shape of which is
concealed by varnished pitch pine
panelling and cupboards. It has
a bathroom-cum-box room lit by
a stained-glass window in the wall

The winter garden

of the stairwell. This room can also be reached from the lower landing.

Simone Horta's bedroom has lost all its original furnishings. Only the recently restored winter garden bears witness to the sense of harmony that these rooms must have produced. When the house was extended, Horta used the extension of the party wall to enable a lateral light to penetrate these new spaces. The small dining room added to the side of the salon, extending the pantry to the bel étage, and the winter garden were fitted with two similar windows. The fact that the house was deeper than the studio enabled Horta to illuminate the bathroom mostly by the same process right from the start.

Lantern above the principal stairwell

For the inhabitants of the house, going up the stairs was always a pleasure comparable to that experienced on a sunny summer's day. The yellow windows obliterate any notion of grey and the fine arabesques of the metal structure reflected to infinity in the mirrors are a feast to the eyes. The staircase is of an extremely light construc-tion, letting light fall right into the heart of the house. The central void gradually expands from the bottom up and as a result the steps become less wide. The interplay of propor-tion changes and where the step is at its narrowest, the banister is at its highest. This subconsciously reas-sures anyone climbing the stairs. By applying a great deal of science,

Glass window in the roof above the lantern

Horta uses the same decorative motif, the curves of which gradually becoming less taut. So that the lantern does not look like a black hole in the evening, the architect mounted a lamp on the banisters, the light from which produces blue tones in the American glass. The sun's glare by day becomes lunar softness by night. The lantern is protected by a glass window installed in the slope of the roof. In the enclosed space between the two, Horta conceals the attachments for the four tie-rods from which the upper section of the stairs is suspended. These tie-rods are bolted into two metal girders anchored in the walls of the stairwell. They also serve to support the banister for the last two flights; the wrought-ironwork is no longer attached to the step, thereby retaining its maximum width.

On the third floor, part of the light from the skylight in the roof escapes laterally through a large window inserted in the wall of the stairwell to provide light for the landing for the three servants' bedrooms.

While still complying with the dimensions stipulated by the communal authorities, Horta managed to squeeze ten levels into his house.

Victor Horta in his office

Reception area of the museum

Lack of documentation means that not much is known of the studio furnishings. We know slightly more only about the floor that Horta reserved for his own use. Connected to the music room, its façade, with its beautifully designed picture windows and frames, gives an indication of its importance. This room could be used as a smoking room, additional reception room or waiting room. Strictly speaking, the back room was the office; Horta worked with his back to the fireplace, looking towards the door to the stairs so as to welcome any colleague who might wish to consult him. Towards 1900 there were about twenty people working in his studio. A telephone box was installed in the stairwell, between the ground floor and the first floor. During the recent restoration works, the original colours on the walls were rediscovered, and two tones of ochre now blend with the wooden stairs, which had to be stripped and varnished. The ground floor of the studio has been transformed into a reception area, with furniture designed by the architect Barbara Van der Wee and the lighting by Henriette Michaux. Only the coffered ceilings are original and have survived successive conversions. They are the decisive factor in creating the desired atmosphere in this space which gives visitors their first impressions of the house.

The cloakroom at the entrance makes it possible to protect the house's delicate wall coverings.

Some of the museum's collection of plaster models are on display in the studio cellars, in other words in the very place where they were made. The scale model of the Palais des Beaux-Arts is the only surviving model of a building. Those of the Hôtel Aubecq and of the Maison du Peuple which are also on show were produced by the Archétype studio for the first one-man exhibition devoted to Horta at the Brussels Palais des Beaux-Arts in 1996. A few architectural fragments from the Maison du Peuple have also found a home in these cellars. They evoke a time when Art Nouveau was still mockingly called *style nouille* and when its most accomplished examples were not considered worth protecting.

First floor of the studio

First floor of the studio

Foot of the monumental stone staircase of the Maison du peuple

Tripod with Cantonese vase

Like most of the artists of his time, Victor Horta was fascinated by Japanese art, an aesthetic shock which goes some way to explaining the original use of his talent from 1893. When they discovered Japanese engravings, western artists were impressed by another way of representing space, by the fluid and undulating line, by the boldness of the centring and by the perception of nature captured in all its manifestations (animal life, plants or atmospheric changes).

The international exhibitions (Japan took part officially for the first time in Paris in 1867), some specialist art galleries and learned authors, such as Louis Gonse and the Goncourt brothers, helped spread Japanese art. Between 1888 and 1891 one such art dealer, Siegfrid Bing, edited a sumptuous review in Paris, *Le Japon artistique,* to which Horta subscribed. The architect met Bing soon after, and in 1895 Bing asked him to draw up plans to convert his gallery into an art shop in Art Nouveau style.

But Horta had other occasions on which to become acquainted with Japanese art. His first important client, Emile Tassel, had a beautiful collection of objets d'art, for which Horta created display cabinets used as transparent partition walls between the landing and the reception room on the bel étage. The mural paintings and the stained-glass window on the first floor of the Hôtel Tassel conjure up the seabed and a landscape painted in the Japanese style. With the money from his first commissions, Horta also soon began to enjoy collecting. A contemporary photograph of his salon in the rue Américaine shows a three-door display cabinet full of lacquer ware, enamel ware and bronze and ivory objets d'art, all apparently more often chosen for their decorative value than for their rare artistic qualities. Continuing an old tradition, Horta enhanced the decorative capacity of certain objects by means of mounts or settings he designed himself; he thus gave them

Garden side salon with the Turin display cabinet containing Japanese objets d'art

a contemporary note ensuring that they could be fully integrated in the décor of a house where nothing escaped his ideas of style. He designed a bronze tripod for a Cantonese stoneware vase and an imitation lacquer, gold-sprayed frame for a piece of embroidery.

The buildings we suggest you explore after your visit to the museum are not open to the public.

1 The Horta Museum
2 Hôtel Tassel
3 Hôtel Solvay
4 Hôtel Max Hallet
5 Maison Vinck
6 Maison Sander Pierron
7 Hôtel Dubois

Hôtel Tassel marks the break with
tradition as far as bourgeois architecture is concerned. The interior
design can be read clearly from the
façade, windows being in propor-
tion to the size of the spaces. All
Tassel's social life can be seen in the
façade: cloakroom and parlour on
either side of the entrance door,
smoking room on the mezzanine
floor, office on the first floor and
study on the second, the rooms
for personal use being situated on
the garden side. Horta uses stone,
a material generally considered too
much of a luxury for a house of this
size. In this case the use of stone
makes it possible to impart a curved
movement to the façade in such a
way as to make a start on the bulge
of the bow window. Horta was the
first to use metal structures in
domestic architecture. Incredibly
slender supports (bracketed corner
irons on the first floor and small
wrought-iron columns on the second) achieve great transparency.
Inside, small wrought-iron columns
and visible iron spans make it possible to do away with some load-
bearing walls. For the bel-étage
landing, Horta exploits the full
width of the plot: the lighting
assumes a special magic as a result
of all the sources, whether visible
or concealed. On either side of the
flight of stairs to the landing, the
stairwell leading to this floor and
the winter garden, both topped

Detail of the bow window

with glass roofs, act as sources of light. Light is also filtered through the stained glass windows of the smoking room that opens like a theatre box onto the void of the large landing or through the transparent partitions that separate the landing from the salon. Horta took care to ensure that the décor was absolutely harmonious and himself conceived the murals that adorn the winter garden and stairwell partitions. The arabesque motifs link the structural elements and the various materials that make up the décor.

Chair (Tassel model with original English fabric)

The Hôtel Solvay looks like a spectacular application of the principles applied to the Hôtel Tassel one year earlier. The rejection of the right angle leads to the use of curves to integrate the projection of the balcony from the bel étage and the large bow windows. Two slender columns, two-floors tall and with metal lintels, help open up the building. Horta drew his inspiration from the traditional composition of the large *hôtels de maître* by installing a carriage entrance. In the middle of a corridor, a double door opens, leading to a vast open space. The kitchen is in the section on the left (garden side) and the cloakroom and parlour are on the right (street side). The main marble staircase divides into two after the first landing: one flight leads to a series of connected rooms (street side), the other to the dining room. These rooms can be opened almost fully onto the void of the stairwell by means of numerous doors. On days when a reception was being held, all the space could be taken in at a glance. The blind stairwell partition is covered by a picture by Théo Van Rysselberghe, *La Lecture dans le parc* (*Reading in the Park,* 1902), in total harmony with the coloured mosaic of the double-fan-shaped lantern glass that brings light to the heart of the house. Here too light comes both from above and from the side. Horta creates a second light source to illuminate the staircase leading to the floors used by the family. The first-floor landing is treated like a salon with a winter garden, its curved floral stained glass being located in the wall of the light source that corresponds to the double-fan-shaped stained glass. Horta was aware he had achieved a monumental work (*Mémoires,* p. 69) because the commission included all the interior décor right up to the last doorknob. The carpets, stained glass, murals and furniture all exhibit the sophisticated harmony so rarely achieved at that time in a commission of this size.

Detail of the carriage entrance

Second-floor gallery

It was inevitable that Victor Horta would get to know Max Hallet. A Freemason, a close friend of Tassel and a member of the Belgian Workers' Party, this lawyer had a long and brilliant political career. He seems to have commissioned furniture from Horta from 1896. In 1902 his father-in-law decided to have a private house built for his daughter and Hallet. Horta designed a house suitable for holding receptions: the connecting salon and dining room give out onto a hall, from which the principal stairway rises, topped with a glass roof. The first flight of stairs leads to a huge landing extended on the garden side by a three-lobed conservatory. The landing is thus transformed into a living space or reception area. Directly alongside the carriage entrance, Horta placed an antechamber connecting the office of the master of the house with the salon. The pantry on the garden side of the ground floor is situated beneath the landing. The first floor is reserved for family use with a large salon flanked by an office at the front and a bedroom on the garden side. Here Horta breaks with the complexity of his previous plans, in which he tried to interweave spaces to produce a spiral route through the house. The façade reflects the calm of the composition: the bow windows on the first floor accentuated by the fluid line of the balcony, whose railings display a repetitive motif; the large skylights; the importance attached to the ground-floor windows in the office and the salon. Here, the beauty of the stonework, the subtle scanning of the consoles and the modillions and the opulence of the window sills on the ground floor are striking. The vitality of early Art Nouveau gives way to a formal elegance that shows Horta returning to his classical training.

For Horta, Emile Vinck was the
spiritual double of Max Hallet
(*Mémoires,* p. 119). A lawyer, member of the Belgian Workers' Party
and senator from 1912, he commissioned the architect to design a
house, less prestigious than that of
Max Hallet, but not so far removed
in terms of layout, with the lawyer's
office to the left of the entrance hall
and a visiting room to the right
which could be used as a cloakroom
on reception days. On the garden
side were a dining room, a music
room and a small, family dining
room. The house has since been
converted. It has been made taller,
which has changed the height of
the big hall and caused the original
lantern to disappear. At the front,
the little picture windows of the
floor beneath the roof have made
way for the windows of a second
floor in its own right. Horta's mark
is visible today mainly in the first-
floor balcony.

This house, built by Horta for one of his close friends, the art critic Sander Pierron, bears comparison with the pavilions of the Brugmann hospital (preliminary plans of 1907). The architect was working to a tight budget that did not permit any 'superfluous' decorative detail. The sets of differently coloured bricks constitute a less expensive decorative ploy. Only the doorframe is finished with sculpted stone. In this very simple façade, which revives a traditional plan (the cellar kitchen appears on the front side), the emphasis is placed on the second floor. The window to Sander Pierron's office resembles a studio stained-glass window: it shows the occupant's artistic qualities. Here Horta seems to equate with Paul Hankar, who had often been approached by artist friends. Horta, however, carried out only a few commissions of this type, his reputation as 'the most expensive architect in town' (*Mémoires,* p. 64) perhaps deterring his less fortunate associates. Nonetheless, this house demonstrates his ability to produce beautiful architecture with great restraint.

The balcony

Door handle

The chimney in the salon

The friendship between Horta and the award-winning sculptor Fernand Dubois arose from a project to decorate the walls of the Hôtel Tassel salon in 'Egyptian style' (*Mémoires,* p. 94). Horta went on to design two buildings for him, a town house and a country house at Sosoye, in the Sambre-Meuse region. It is extremely illuminating to compare the Hôtel Dubois with the architect's own house and studio in the rue Américaine. In the case of the Hôtel Dubois, the house and study are connected. Although the large window reveals the sculptor's studio, the general impression is one of a sense of unity between the two functions. It is true that Dubois had no need for a team of colleagues who could have intruded upon his family life. The succession of different-shaped picture windows above the entrance door indicates the stairwell. Overhead lighting is restricted to the studio and is not marked in the section reserved for habitation, which has two rooms per floor. The harmony of this asymmetrical façade, executed entirely in blue stone, lies in the creations dating from the 1890s, but the absence of any outstanding movement shows Horta in search of a new, more refined way.

Wrought-iron element from the staircase of the Maison du peuple incorporated in the new staircase of the cellar

Actes du Colloque Horta, 20 November 1996 in the Palais des Académies in Brussels. Published by the Académie Royale de Belgique, Classe des Beaux-Arts, 1997.

Françoise AUBRY (J. EVRARD and Chr. BASTIN, photography), *Victor Horta à Bruxelles,* Brussels, Racine, 1996.

Françoise AUBRY, *Victor Horta and Brussels,* in *Art Nouveau 1890–1914* (ed. Paul GREENHALGH), London, V & A Publications, 2000, p. 274–285.

Françoise AUBRY and Jos VANDENBREEDEN (J. EVRARD and Chr. BASTIN, photography), *Art Nouveau in Belgium. Architecture & Interior Design,* Tielt, Lannoo, 1991.

Frans BOENDERS, Anne HUSTACHE, Steven JACOBS, *Victor Horta. Le Palais des Beaux-Arts de Bruxelles,* Brussels, Crédit Communal and Ghent, Snoeck-Ducaju, 1996.

Franco BORSI and Paolo PORTOGHESI, *Victor Horta,* Brussels, Vokaer, 1970 (reprint 1990 with new illustrations and some additions).

Jean DELHAYE and Françoise AUBRY, *La Maison du Peuple de Victor Horta,* Brussels, Atelier Vokaer, 1987.

David DERNIE and Alastair CAREW-COX, *Victor Horta,* London, Academy Editions, 1995.

Françoise DIERKENS-AUBRY (J. EVRARD and Chr. BASTIN, photography), *The Horta Museum. Brussels Saint-Gilles,* Brussels, Crédit Communal, 1990 (Musea Nostra).

Françoise DIERKENS-AUBRY, 'Victor Horta, architecte de monuments civils et funéraires,' in Bulletin de la Commission Royale des Monuments et des Sites, XIII, 1986, p. 37–101.

A. HOPPENBROUWERS, J. VANDENBREEDEN, J. BRUGGEMANS, R. SOMERS, *Victor Horta. Architectonographie,* Brussels, Confédération Nationale de la Construction, 1975.

Horta, Art Nouveau to Modernism (ed. Françoise AUBRY and Jos VANDENBREEDEN; Reiner LAUTWEIN, photography), Ghent, Ludion. Published on the occasion of the exhibition 'Horta' in the Palais des Beaux-Arts in Brussels, from 4 October 1996 to 5 January 1997.

Anne HUSTACHE and Françoise AUBRY (A. CAREW-COX, photography), *Victor Horta. Maisons de campagne,* Brussels, Edition du Musée Horta, 1994.

Yolande OOSTENS-WITTAMER, *L'hôtel Solvay. The Solvay House,* Louvain-la-Neuve, Institut Supérieur d'Archéologie et d'Histoire de l'Art, 1980. 2 volumes.

IDEM, *Horta en Amérique.*

Décembre 1915–Janvier 1919, Brussels-Hamburg, Editions Lebeer-Hossmann and Commission française de la Culture de l'Agglomération de Bruxelles, 1986.

IDEM (Oswald PAUWELS, photography), *L'hôtel Solvay,* Paris, Diane de Selliers, 1996.

Victor Horta. Architetto e Designer (1861–1947). Opere dal Musée Horta di Bruxelles, L'Arcaedizioni. Exhibition catalogue. Ferrara, Gallerie Civiche del Palazzo dei Diamanti. 21 December 1991–1 March 1992.

Victor Horta. Mémoires (ed. Cécile DULIÈRE). Ministère de la Communauté française de Belgique. Administration du Patrimoine Culturel, 1985.

© 2001 Ludion Gent-Amsterdam and Françoise Aubry
© 2001 Victor Horta, SOFAM Belgium
© Bastin & Evrard s.p.r.l.
Translation: Harriet Horsfield in association with First Edition Translations Ltd, Cambridge, UK
Design: Antoon De Vylder, Herentals
Typesetting: De Diamant Pers, Herentals
Colour separations and printing: Die Keure, Bruges
D/2001/6328/44
ISBN: 90-5544-384-0